Whatever Happens to Kittens?

By BILL HALL

Pictures by VIRGINIA PARSONS

MERRIGOLD PRESS • NEW YORK

© 1967 Merrigold Press, Racine, Wisconsin 53402. All rights reserved. Printed in the U.S.A.
No part of this book may be reproduced or copied in any form without written permission from the
publisher. All trademarks are the property of Merrigold Press. ISBN: 0-307-10940-2
MCMXCII

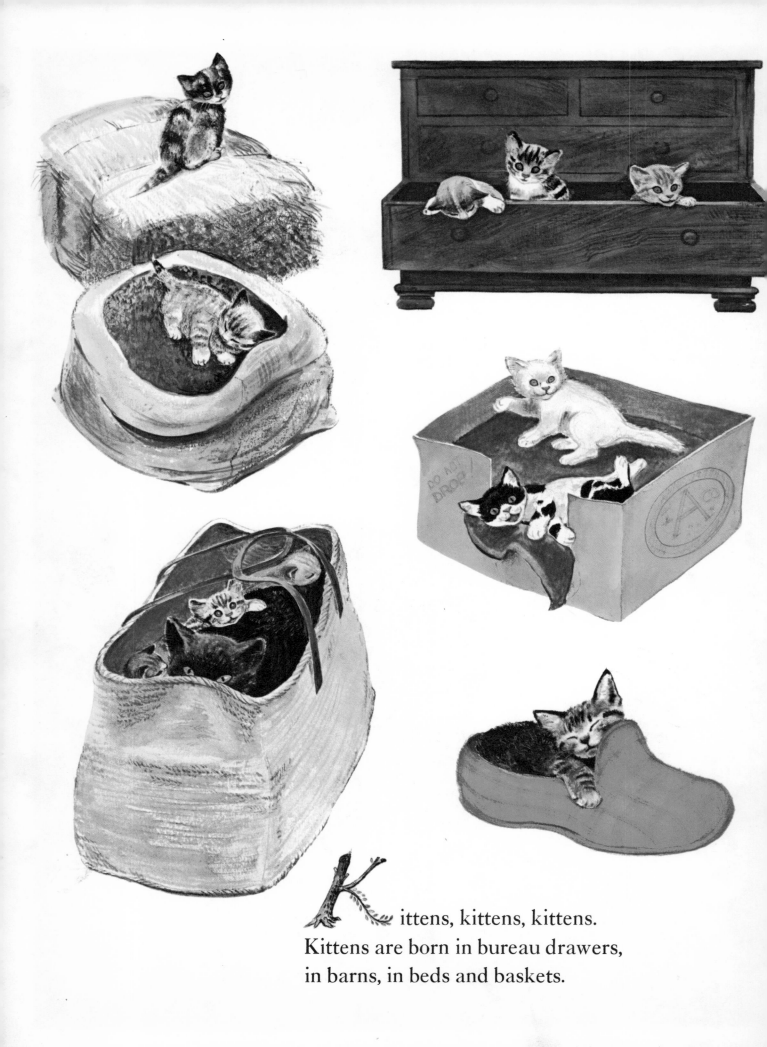

ittens, kittens, kittens.
Kittens are born in bureau drawers,
in barns, in beds and baskets.

Kittens are born everywhere, every day.
Kittens, kittens, kittens.
Whatever happens to them all?

Before anything happens to her kittens,
the mother cat peers and sniffs about,
looking for a safe place to have them.

There! She has found the place.
She lies down. She cleans herself. Mother cat
is getting ready for her new family.

One. Two. Three. This mother cat has three kittens.
The mother can take care of that many very nicely,
feeding them and keeping them clean.

At first, the kittens were three tiny balls of fuzz,
unable to see. But soon they can see. They are
growing bigger and getting their coats.

Sometimes the mother takes them to a safer place, one by one. Maybe she is carrying them to show them off to people—she is so proud of them.

Sometimes they arch their backs and open their
mouths to look fierce. Sometimes, right in the middle
of a jump, they go plop! and fall asleep.

After they have eaten, and played, and slept
every day for a few more weeks—after they have
learned everything their mother can teach them—
they are ready for new homes, new places where
they can eat and play and sleep and purr.

Whatever happens to them then?
They have names now.
Wiggs lives with people
in an apartment house.

Taffy lives with people in the country.

And Mittens lives with people near the ocean.

They are big cats. And they still eat and play
and sleep and purr.

Sometimes they clean themselves
even when they are not dirty, just for fun.

They live with people who like them, and they like
the people. That's what happened to these kittens.

But other things happen to other kittens.
Whatever happened to this kitten?

The firemen had to save her.

Whatever happened to this kitten?

He helps in a butcher shop.

Whatever happened to these kittens?

They are wild tigers.
They live in the jungle.

Cats smile, and cats cry.

Most cats have eighteen toes
and some cats have no tails.

Sometimes cats seem to be in a far away dream
though they look you in the eye.

They purr and hiss and help to open packages.

Cats are cats who once were kittens.